"Christians are pressed by very real questions. How does Scripture structure a church, order worship, organize ministry, and define biblical leadership? Those are just examples of the questions that are answered clearly, carefully, and winsomely in this new series from 9Marks. I am so thankful for this ministry and for its incredibly healthy and hopeful influence in so many faithful churches. I eagerly commend this series."

R. Albert Mohler Jr., President, The Southern Baptist Theological Seminary

"Sincere questions deserve thoughtful answers. If you're not sure where to start in answering these questions, let this series serve as a diving board into the pool. These minibooks are winsomely to-the-point and great to read together with one friend or one hundred friends."

Gloria Furman, author, *Missional Motherhood* and *The Pastor's Wife*

"As a pastor, I get asked lots of questions. I'm approached by unbelievers seeking to understand the gospel, new believers unsure about next steps, and maturing believers wanting help answering questions from their Christian family, friends, neighbors, or coworkers. It's in these moments that I wish I had a book to give them that was brief, answered their questions, and pointed them in the right direction for further study. Church Questions is a series that provides just that. Each booklet tackles one question in a biblical, brief, and practical manner. The series may be called Church Questions, but it could be called 'Church Answers.' I intend to pick these up by the dozens and give them away regularly. You should too."

Juan R. Sanchez, Senior Pastor, High Pointe Baptist Church, Austin, Texas

How Can Our Church Find a Faithful Pastor?

Church Questions

How Can Our Church Find a Faithful Pastor?

Mark Dever

CROSSWAY®

WHEATON, ILLINOIS

How Can Our Church Find a Faithful Pastor?

Copyright © 2020 by 9Marks

Published by Crossway
        1300 Crescent Street
        Wheaton, Illinois 60187

All rights reserved. No part of this publication may be reproduced, stored in a retrieval system, or transmitted in any form by any means, electronic, mechanical, photocopy, recording, or otherwise, without the prior permission of the publisher, except as provided for by USA copyright law. Crossway® is a registered trademark in the United States of America.

Cover design: Jordan Singer

First printing 2020

Printed in the United States of America

Scripture quotations are from the ESV® Bible (The Holy Bible, English Standard Version®), copyright © 2001 by Crossway, a publishing ministry of Good News Publishers. Used by permission. All rights reserved.

All emphases in Scripture quotations have been added by the author.

Trade paperback ISBN: 978-1-4335-7020-9
ePub ISBN: 978-1-4335-7023-0
PDF ISBN: 978-1-4335-7021-6
Mobipocket 978-1-4335-7022-3

Library of Congress Cataloging-in-Publication Data

Names: Dever, Mark, author.
Title: How can our church find a faithful pastor? / Mark Dever.
Description: Wheaton, Illinois : Crossway, [2020] | Series: Church questions | Includes bibliographical references and index.
Identifiers: LCCN 2020003078 (print) | LCCN 2020003079 (ebook) | ISBN 9781433570209 (trade paperback) | ISBN 9781433570216 (pdf) | ISBN 9781433570223 (mobi) | ISBN 9781433570230 (epub)
Subjects: LCSH: Clergy—Appointment, call, and election. | Pastoral search committees. | Elders (Church officers)
Classification: LCC BV664 .D474 2020 (print) | LCC BV664 (ebook) | DDC 254—dc23
LC record available at https://lccn.loc.gov/2020003078
LC ebook record available at https://lccn.loc.gov/2020003079

Crossway is a publishing ministry of Good News Publishers.

BP		29	28	27	26	25	24	23	22	21	20
15	14	13	12	11	10	9	8	7	6	5	4	3	2	1

He gave the apostles, the prophets, the evangelists, the shepherds and teachers, to equip the saints for the work of ministry.

Ephesians 4:11–12

We tend to esteem someone's final words. So consider David's final words from 2 Samuel 23:3–4:

> The God of Israel has spoken;
>> the Rock of Israel has said to me:
> When one rules justly over men,
>> ruling in the fear of God,
> he dawns on them like the morning light,
>> like the sun shining forth on a
>>> cloudless morning,
>> like rain that makes grass to sprout
>>> from the earth.

Spiritual authority wielded in a way that honors God brings flourishing and life. Conversely, spiritual authority wielded dishonorably wreaks havoc and devastation. Sadly, many Christians know this from experience. Far from the morning dawn or a much-needed dew, ungodly or ill-equipped pastors bring darkness and destruction to their churches. They hurt people. But a godly pastor, a true shepherd, is one of Christ's greatest gifts to his people (Eph. 4:11; cf. Acts 20:28).

Friend, if your church is currently looking for a pastor, pray that God would send your church a man who knows how to wield authority—not for his own sake but for the spiritual good of others.

Your church needs a godly pastor.

In this little book, I'll provide some biblical and practical advice on how to find a godly pastor. We'll examine who should lead the search for the new pastor, what to look for in a pastor, and then consider some practical steps on how to move forward.[1] But before we begin, let me take a moment to address the pastors on their way out. Despite what many think, the outgoing senior pastor plays a critical role in the success of your church's transition to the next pastor.

A Quick Word to Current Senior Pastors

To any pastors who may be reading, let me remind you—yes, you!—of your own responsibilities in helping your church find your successor.[2]

Unless you're pastoring your church when the Lord comes back, you will always be preparing your congregation for the next man. Sadly, many pastors seem utterly indifferent to how their churches will fare after they've gone.

But one of the most important parts of a pastor's ministry is helping to secure a sound man to follow him. Robert Murray M'Cheyne once told his congregation: "Changes are coming. Every eye before me shall soon be dim in death. Another pastor shall feed this flock, another singer lead the Psalm, another flock shall fill this fold."[3]

Brother pastor, do you speak to your congregation like that? Do you make them aware of the speedy passage of time and the obligations that puts on us? How are you seeking your congregation's blessing and benefit beyond your own ministry there? Do you truly love the sheep or just the paycheck?

Let me quickly suggest three things you ought to be doing right now to prepare your church to transition well to the next man.

First, prepare your church for the next pastor by teaching your congregation that godly elders are a gift to the church.[4] In other words, raise up other leaders. As you establish elders, remind your people to be thankful for each of their shepherds, not just the senior pastor. Go out of your way to ensure that you build your ministry around the Bible and not around your own cult of personality. Diminish the number of times you preach so that other capable men in your congregation can fill the pulpit. This will help your congregation get accustomed to hearing preaching that's not yours. Cultivate in your people an appetite for *sound preaching*, not just *your preaching*.

Second, prepare for your transition by making sure you're financially prepared to no longer have your current job. I cannot tell you how many times I've heard a pastor keep his job when he feels burnt-out because he doesn't know how else he's going to make a living. That should never happen.

Finally, when it comes time to leave, suggest someone (either from inside or outside the church) that you think would be a suitable replacement. This is faithfulness, not interference. Shepherding your church through this decision will be one of the last ways to *love* your congregation. Of course, sometimes the Lord calls shepherds away swiftly, like when a man dies. Generally speaking, however, a shepherd shouldn't assume his charge is complete until he does everything within his power to secure a worthy successor.

Who Should Lead the Search?

Let's turn now to consider *how* a church should find its next pastor. The most pressing question: Who should lead this search? Most churches, at least in America, appoint pastoral search committees to this task.

I know many dear, godly folks who have served in such committees around the country and even around the world. This task is momentous, and many search committee members give their time prayerfully and with a sense of being given a sacred privilege. *Thank you to those who have approached this task lovingly and dutifully!*

Questioning the Search Committee Model

And yet, I encourage churches *not* to create search committees to find their next pastor. Let me explain why.

If churches were healthier, we'd never need to call together such a committee. A faithful pastor recognizes that even if he's at his church until he dies, he's still only temporary. He understands his responsibility to raise up other pastors and elders. With faithful godly pastors and elders leading a church, these men should have the resources and training necessary to find a faithful pastor who reflects the character of a true shepherd found in the pages of Scripture.

Sadly, too many pastors have failed to discharge this crucial responsibility. They've failed to raise up other pastors and elders. As a result, many congregations have been left with no choice but to create a committee.

The basic problem with search committees is that they are typically built to do the wrong thing. They're built—again, typically, not always—to represent different portions of the congregation in the process of finding a pastor. A church appoints some women to the committee to represent the women's perspective, men to represent the men, young and old to represent the young and the old, the businessman, the deacon, the musicians, and so forth. In other words, search committees are built on the principle of representation.

There's nothing wrong with incorporating the interests of different kinds of people, but let's not put the cart before the horse. *The most important criterion that the people responsible for nominating the next pastor should meet is an ability to represent the "interests" of the Bible, not the interests of different kinds of people.* Simply put, this group of people needs to understand Scripture well—how to "rightly [handle] the word of truth" (2 Tim. 2:15)—so that they will prioritize what Scripture prioritizes in looking for a pastor.

Yes, these individuals *should* be interested in finding someone who knows how to love and serve men and women, young and old, and every other group in the church. After all, Paul left his protégé Timothy many instructions on how to pastor different kinds of people. But this group must approach their job asking first what Scripture says. Only then will they have the wisdom and experience necessary for differentiating between various candidates.

So if you don't use a search committee, who in your church should lead the search to find a new pastor?

Let the Elders Lead

If your church has other pastors and elders, let them lead. After all, God has charged these men with leadership. Just a quick word here on defining these terms. According to Scripture, "pastor" and "elder" are simply two terms to refer to the same office. If your church doesn't have lay-pastors or lay-elders, chances are that you still have identified one or more "pastors" who are likely providing leadership for the church. Even as you look for a new pastor, let these men take the lead.

To be sure, the New Testament does teach that the congregation as a whole has responsibility for its membership, discipline, and doctrine (Matt. 18:15–20; 1 Cor. 5; Gal. 1:6–10). So there seems to be good biblical precedent for viewing the congregation as owning the *final* responsibility for recognizing its leaders (Acts 6:3). Yet even within this congregational framework, God charges elders to teach, shepherd, and lead, and he charges the congregation to submit to its elders (1 Tim. 3:1–7; Titus 1:5–9; Heb. 13:17; 1 Pet. 5:1–5).

With this basic structure in mind, here are a few reasons why elders should lead this process (rather than a search committee comprised of a demographic cross-section of the congregation).

First, elders are best qualified to assess a man's preaching and teaching. The Bible charges elders to teach sound doctrine and to ensure that no false doctrine is propagated in the church (Titus 1:9). This explains why all elders must be "able to teach" (1 Tim. 3:2). Further, since a pastor is simply an elder who is set aside to preach full-time, his most important job is to preach God's word faithfully (2 Tim. 2:15; 4:2). The soundness of a man's preaching is absolutely central to the soundness of his pastoring, and elders are the most qualified to judge a man's preaching.

Second, elders are best qualified to assess a man's character. Another crucial issue when considering a potential pastor is the man's character, and here again the elders are qualified to lead.

Elders are men whom the church has recognized as possessing exemplary character (1 Tim. 3:1–7; Titus 1:5–9). Through their godly character, elders serve as examples for the whole flock (Heb. 13:7; 1 Pet. 5:3). As they teach, disciple, counsel, and chase down errant sheep, the elders share many of the same day-to-day ministry burdens as the senior pastor.

It's also the elders who may well have had confidential conversations with members of the congregation, such that they would best recognize which issues a new pastor would face as well as any matters that might disqualify a man from eldership. By virtue of regularly having such conversations, they're probably most prepared to have careful conversations with any prospective pastoral candidate. They should also have a more practiced ability to detect weak spots.

By both qualification and experience, a church's elders are best able to assess a potential pastor's character. This *doesn't* mean, however, that the elders shouldn't also pursue character references on a potential pastor, especially if the candidate comes from outside the church.

Third, elders are charged to raise up other elders. In 2 Timothy 2:2 Paul writes, "And what you have heard from me in the presence of many witnesses entrust to faithful men, who will be able to teach others also." God intends for those who teach the word in the church to raise up others who will also be able to teach the word. While Scripture doesn't tell us whether Timothy held the office of elder in the church in Ephesus, this verse clearly seems to establish a pattern that elders are to follow today. After all, if Timothy was to teach reliable men who would be able to teach others, then those men would have understood from Timothy's example that they were to raise up others themselves.

It bears repetition: elders should always raise up other elders. So what about when the church needs to find an elder who is particularly gifted in preaching, whom we often call a "senior pastor"? The best group of people to find that individual is a church's elders—biblically qualified men who are already in the habit of recognizing and cultivating godly men to be elders. So when the need arises for a church to find a particularly gifted elder to set aside to preach full-time, shouldn't the group who has already devoted themselves to this task take the lead?

Finding a new pastor requires wisdom, discernment, theological acuity, and more. If you've got elders, this is when you need them most!

What If Our Church Doesn't Have Elders?

Of course, your church may not currently have elders. If that's the case, don't be discouraged. I'll continue addressing pastoral search committees throughout the rest of this book. If you're currently on a search committee, consider how you can employ the bigger principles in this booklet to find a faithful pastor—preferably one that will raise up other elders so that you won't encounter this problem in the future.

For now, try to identify the most "elder-like" individuals in your congregation—those with a track record of proven character and sound theological conviction. Perhaps your deacons can serve in this role since many of the character qualifications for elders are also required of deacons. Ask mature men in your congregation to lead the pastoral search and encourage them to seek the Bible's interests and not their own.

What to Look For in a Pastor

Now that we've considered who ought to lead the church in its pastoral search, let's consider *what* to look for in a pastor.

1. Find a Man Committed to Expositional Preaching

If someone happily accepts the authority of God's word, yet in practice does not preach expositionally, he will never preach more than he already knows.

Don't employ a pastor who uses Scripture as a pretext for his own ideas. Commitment to the authority of Scripture means making the point of the text the point of the sermon. Granting spiritual oversight of the flock to someone who doesn't in practice show a commitment to hear and to teach God's word will be spiritually disastrous. The church will slowly be conformed to his mind, rather than God's.

2. Find a Man Committed to Sound Doctrine and a Biblical Understanding of the Gospel

Find a man who both affirms the authority of Scripture *and* reads it carefully. Pursue a pastor-theologian, one who seeks to understand every passage in its proper context.

Ask him what he believes about the character of God, human nature, the work of Christ, and the nature of conversion. These topics are enormously important, not only for biblical fidelity but for facing pastoral issues that constantly arise in the church.

Furthermore, a biblical understanding of the gospel should be at the heart of your future pastor's commitment to sound doctrine. He must understand that every human needs his or her sins forgiven—and that this forgiveness is only available through the substitutionary death of Christ.

3. Find a Man with a Biblical Understanding of Conversion and Evangelism

Conversion isn't something we do; it is an act of God. Conversion certainly *includes* our making a sincere and self-conscious decision to follow Christ, but it's more than that. Scripture clearly teaches that we turn to Christ only when God supernaturally grants us spiritual life, replacing our hearts of stone with hearts of flesh.

Charles Spurgeon humorously conveyed this truth with a story about Rowland Hill, a famous eighteenth-century English preacher. Spurgeon notes,

A drunken man came up to Rowland Hill, one day, and said, "I am one of your converts, Mr. Hill." "I daresay you are," replied that shrewd and sensible preacher; "but you are none of the Lord's, or you would not be drunk." To this practical test we must bring all our work.[5]

Sadly, many churches are full of people who, at some point in their lives, made a sincere commitment to follow Christ but who evidently have not experienced the radical change the Bible describes as conversion.

A pastor who understands conversion will have a sound philosophy of evangelism. Evangelism is simply presenting the good news freely and trusting God to bring conversions. If your future pastor views conversion as merely a sincere commitment at any given point, then he'll be more likely to press people using hasty and unbiblical means.

True faith is a supernatural gift of God, one that produces good works (James 2:14–26) and endures in holiness (Matt. 24:13). Yes, your future pastor should care about, plead with, and persuade sinners. But he should do so from a place of peaceful confidence in God's sovereignty, not out of a frantic sense that conversion depends on his rhetorical ingenuity or his implementing the right program.

If your future pastor is coming from a church with a sizable discrepancy between its membership and its attendance, carefully inquire about his understanding of conversion and evangelism. Ask him what practices created such a large number of people who claim to be "members," yet are entirely uninvolved in the life of the church.

Find a pastor who understands that the decision to follow Christ is urgent, costly, and worth it.

4. Find a Man Committed to a Biblical Understanding of Church Membership and Church Discipline

Church membership and discipline mark out the people of God from the world. They define the identity of a particular local church. A pastor committed to church membership recognizes that he and his fellow elders are responsible for the souls of those who have covenanted themselves to their local church (Heb. 13:17).

Regrettably, many pastors view church membership rolls as a way to gauge their success in ministry—the higher the numbers, the greater the sign of God's blessing. But this is misguided and grossly unbiblical. A true pastor will care not that a church's membership is large but that every individual member understands the gospel and is spiritually thriving. He won't care about a growing number of people, but rather a number of people growing. He will recognize that the church's membership roll identifies those he is responsible to shepherd, pray for, teach, warn, disciple, and love.

Similarly, your future pastor should be committed to church discipline. Church discipline is clearly taught in Scripture. It's how a church maintains the purity of its witness, guards the gospel, and warns false converts of the dangers of self-deception. To be sure, church discipline

is counter-cultural and often emotionally tax-
ing. For that reason, find a pastor who is both
compassionate and courageous enough to follow Scripture.

5. Find a Man Committed to Discipling Others

Pastors have an obligation to help others follow
Jesus. They succeed at this task when they're
more committed to the spiritual well-being of
others than to worldly metrics of success. Any
pastor who cares well for his church will value
and model healthy discipling relationships.

6. Find a Man Who Understands and Is Convinced of the New Testament Practice of Having a Plurality of Elders

A good pastor doesn't want to hoard authority;
he wants to give it away to others. He wants to
raise up other godly men to share the load of
shepherding such that God's people are better
served. A team of qualified elders rounds out
any pastor's gifts, supports him in the work of
the ministry, keeps him from rash or foolish

actions, and opens the opportunity to create a culture of shepherding. If a man seems unwilling to raise up other elders, then it is likely he doesn't have a clear grasp of what Scripture teaches about the church—or, worse, he may still be clinging to some unsanctified self-centeredness that values personal authority over the good of others.

Moving Forward: Best Practices for Finding Your Next Pastor

In light of everything we've covered, let me offer these next steps.[6]

1. Prepare

Once again, it's impossible to overemphasize just how important it is for the current pastor and the elders to prepare the congregation for transition. Both in your teaching and in your philosophy of ministry, cultivate a congregation with the maturity to transition from one senior pastor to the next. Cultivate an allegiance to Scripture, not to any particular pastor.

2. Agree

The senior pastor and the other elders should agree on a transition plan. They should discuss the date on which the current pastor will cease being responsible for the preaching ministry of the church. They should talk about the date by which they'd like to begin a search for their next preacher. Clearly agreeing on these benchmarks allows for a smoother transition.

Of course, situations vary. Perhaps the current minister moves on to another church, or perhaps he or the other elders can sense he's wearing out. If that's the case, he needs to start thinking about changing his role. Honest, sensitive, and open conversation about this among the elders is *always* helpful. Once replaced, the former pastor may need to move on or he may be able to constructively stay on after the new man is preaching. I've heard and seen many examples in both directions.

Some pastors live by the cardinal rule that if you have had a good ministry, you must be able to stay in your church under the leadership of the next man. Others believe that once you finish, you've got to get out of there. I don't think a single rule applies in every situation.

3. Search

Sometimes the elders already have in mind the man who should become the next pastor—often a candidate who is already a member or an elder of the church. An internal candidate is often the best fit, particularly since he may already be known and loved by the congregation and the church already trusts his character.

In other situations, elders or the search committee will need to gather names of potential candidates and deliberate about them.

As you consider possible candidates, be careful to avoid the following pitfalls:

Avoid negative influence from self-interested denominational leaders. If your church belongs to a denomination where the authority of Scripture is under attack, consider very carefully the interests that denominational leaders have in making sure you get a pastor who's acceptable to them. They may have unsavory theological or political reasons to want to install certain people in your congregation, and they can exercise undue influence on a committee of lay people who humbly want to defer to "the professionals."

Avoid a beauty pageant mentality. What does this mean? It's simple. Too often, search committees will look at a number of different candidates, rank them, and conduct their own version of a pastor's tournament of champions. I understand, everyone wants the best for his or her church. But your church doesn't need the best preacher in your state. You simply need a faithful man who loves the word of God and can shepherd the people of God. Don't turn your search process into a pastoral beauty pageant.

Also, you don't want to fall prey to the same worldly thinking God repeatedly condemned in the Old Testament. The Israelites wanted Saul as their king because he was tall and looked like the kings of the nations. As you search for a pastor, avoid the temptation to value worldly markers of success as Israel did. Remember God's words to Samuel, "Do not look on his appearance or

on the height of his stature. . . . For the LORD
sees not as man sees: man looks on the outward
appearance, but the LORD looks on the heart"
(1 Sam. 16:7).

*Avoid prioritizing experience and age over
character and giftedness.* Search committees tend
to be too risk-averse. Again, the very nature of
search committees is to represent the congregation, which means they're designed to look
for a candidate that pleases everyone. And the
only way to satisfy *everyone*—often—is to find
a middle-of-the-road, milquetoast candidate.

Most commonly, committees prefer experience over character and giftedness. It's true,
young pastors can be problematic. They tend
to have great acuity but poor depth perception.
They see truth sharply and often accurately, but
they don't have experience in knowing how to
implement things well. But that's not true of
every young pastor. If he's truly humble, then he
will seek wisdom from older, godly men. That's
a sign of a good leader.

God raises up young men who watch their
life and doctrine closely and are gifted to teach

his word publicly. Paul himself supported a young pastor named Timothy, encouraging him: "Let no one despise you for your youth, but set the believers an example in speech, in conduct, in love, in faith, in purity" (1 Tim. 4:12).

Don't overlook younger pastors. Hire them when they're a cub. Let them chew things up around the house for a while, and you'll have a lion that loves you for life. Young pastors make mistakes. But young pastors—if they're called and equipped by God—can stay for a long time and enjoy decades of fruitful ministry. Embrace this long-term perspective.

Your church might need an older pastor who can give you five years of his life before he retires. Your church might need a younger pastor that can serve you for fifty years. But make this decision according to character and gifting—not experience. To put it bluntly, don't follow the practice of hundreds of churches and make "five years of pastoral experience" a prerequisite.

Avoid an inordinate hunger for résumés. Instead of collecting hundreds of resumes, wouldn't it be easier and more immediately productive to get a single reference from a trusted pastor? If there's no one in your congregation suited to be a regular teacher of God's word, then find a church you like, with a pastoral ministry you like, and approach that pastor for a suggested candidate. Pursue that person, and you'll save yourself a lot of time and energy.

Avoid "pastor hunting." I've heard about search committees that have secretly traveled to other churches, hoping to observe a pastor in his natural habitat in order to see how he operates—all unbeknownst to the present congregation with whom they are worshiping. These committees are "pastor hunting."

One Sunday morning, a committee came hunting for me. I knew they were there, so I asked them to stand so our church could pray for them in their search for a new pastor. Don't worry; I had told them I would do this, though they didn't believe me!

I also remember talking to one search committee about various folks they were considering—each of whom were flourishing in their current churches. I asked them to consider carefully why they wanted these men to leave such flourishing ministries. After all, why should we think God loves *our* congregation more than the one whose pastor we want to take?

Avoid fixating on credentials and other unbiblical criteria. Many search committees see degrees as the common currency of pastoral proficiency. But such artificial criteria can hide choice servants of God. While I generally encourage young men to train at a seminary, some of the best pastors I know don't have an MDiv, or even a BA. To put it bluntly, don't follow the practice of hundreds of churches and make an MDiv a prerequisite for hiring your next pastor.

Similarly, don't create other unbiblical criteria for evaluating a pastor. For instance, many search committees won't consider any man who isn't married. But many of the best pastors in church history were single men—Richard Sibbes, Charles Simeon, John Stott, and of course, the apostle Paul.

Finally, avoid preferring a winning personality over a man with a godly character. Find a man who tells you the truth, not one who flatters you. Find a man who is humble and transparent. Find someone who benefits those who spend time with him. Find someone who understands authority, discipling, mercy, and the joy of evangelism—among a host of other things. Find a man with both conviction and compassion.

4. Investigate

Once you've settled on a potential candidate, ask probing questions about the man's character, theology, and philosophy of ministry. If the candidate is coming from outside, the elders should listen to his sermons in person or online. If possible, the elders can listen together to a sermon online and discuss it without the preacher present.

Simply, get to know your candidate and his philosophy of ministry as best as you possibly can.

Here are some questions you should ask a potential candidate:

- Do you agree with everything in this church's statement of faith?

- Do you think there is anything missing in the statement of faith that needs to be added?
- What is the gospel?
- How do you understand what Scripture teaches about the role of women in the church?
- Do you preach topical or expository sermons?
- What do you think Scripture teaches as the pastor's primary responsibility?
- How and when should a church practice church discipline?
- What is evangelism and how would you cultivate evangelism in the church?
- How would you describe your own spiritual health and the health of your family?
- What sins do you struggle with the most?[7]

5. Decide

The elders or search committee should decide on a candidate and move forward provisionally with one name. Be willing to drop him from consideration if it becomes clear that he wouldn't be a good pastor for your church. At that point, just propose another name and repeat this process until a final candidate emerges.

6. Preach, Pray, and Talk

At this point the elders or search committee should pursue an even deeper understanding of the candidate. They should listen to more of his preaching, discuss his theological commitments further, and continue to pray for God's guidance.

If the man is currently serving as a pastor, the elders should ask why this pastor of another church is even considering leaving his current church. They should ask if his church knows that he's considering another possibility. Especially with the elders, the prospective pastor should discuss his theology and his philosophy of ministry.

7. Recommend

At this point, the candidate is made public. The elders or search committee can invite the candidate to preach. He should also meet with church members in various settings and be willing to answer questions from the congregation. After these meetings, the elders can formally recommend that the church call this person to be its pastor.

Let me reiterate: only pursue one candidate at a time. Don't make your pastoral search an NCAA tournament, with multiple candidates preaching to the congregation and trying to excel above the competition.

8. Consider

The congregation should have some time to consider the man brought before them. The amount of time will vary. It could be two weeks, two months, or another reasonable period of time. Even if the congregation has heard him preach during the months leading up to the announcement, it would be irresponsible not to give your congregation time to think, pray, and reflect on the choice of this man as their next pastor (cf. Prov. 15:28; 18:13, 17; 1 Tim. 5:22; Rev. 2:2).

9. Vote

The congregation should vote to affirm the candidate as their pastor. I take this as an implication of the responsibility that the congregation clearly has in the New Testament for bad preachers. For example, in Galatians 1:8–9, Paul effectively says, "Don't listen to me if I come and preach to you another gospel." The congregation must be able to affirm its own pastors and elders.

10. Welcome

You want to end up with a pastor who is happily settled and well taken care of. I've too often heard church leaders say about their pastor: "We'll keep him poor, and God will keep him humble." That's a short-term vision of the ministry, and a great way to turn the pastor's kids against Christianity. It's also an atrociously ungodly attitude to have toward your new pastor. Care for him as you would a family member (1 Tim. 5:8, 17–19).

When he arrives, welcome him with a good level of financial support but also with patience.

Remember that a new pastor is just like the bananas you buy at the store—he needs time to ripen and prove himself. When you first get him, he's a little green. Give him some time. Over the weeks, months, and years, his preaching will improve. He'll grow as a pastor, and you'll also get more used to his preaching. He'll have opportunities to serve and to endear himself through baptisms, weddings, and funerals.

11. Encourage

The new pastor will eventually begin looking for his own successor, of course (2 Tim. 2:2). But one thing that will help him to do that with joy is the encouragement that you give him by sharing some of the ways you have benefited under his ministry. Galatians 6:6 and 1 Timothy 5:17 describe the type of encouragement you ought to give to him: pray for him and pay for him. Be generous with him so he can set a model of generosity to others. If you don't trust his character enough to be generous with him, then you shouldn't hire him in the first place.

Encourage him and receive him as a gift from Christ to your church.

A Decision You Won't Regret

Calling a faithful and godly pastor is a decision you'll never regret.[8]

Edward Griffin was a faithful Presbyterian pastor of a church for many years. During his last message to his congregation, when they were installing his successor, Griffin said:

> For your own sake, and your children's sake, cherish and revere him whom you have chosen to be your pastor. Already he loves you; and he will soon love you as "bone of his bone, and flesh of his flesh." It will be equally your duty and your interest to make his labors as pleasant to him as possible. Do not demand too much. Do not require visits too frequent. Should he spend, in this way, half of the time which some demand, he must wholly neglect his studies, if not sink early under the burden. Do not report to him all the unkind

things which may be said against him; nor
frequently, in his presence, allude to opposition, if opposition should arise. Though
he is a minister of Christ, consider that he
has the feelings of a man.[9]

Brothers and sisters, pastoral authority is
a good and glorious gift from God. In a fallen
world, we tend to think authority is irrevocably
bad. Certainly, abuses of authority are among
the worst blasphemies against God. But we also
intuitively know that every kid wants to be on the
team with the good coach. Everyone wants to be
in the company with the good boss. Everyone
wants to be in the family with the good parents.

Why? Because good authority blesses those
underneath it. God designed us to flourish and
be fruitful under godly authority. Good authority is not fundamentally for those exercising the
authority. It's for the blessing of those under that
authority.

That's the point of David's final words—and
it's why the choice of your church's next pastor is
so vitally important. May God grant you wisdom.

Notes

1. Portions of this booklet are from Mark Dever, "What's Wrong with Search Committees? Part 1 of 2 on Finding a Pastor," 9Marks website, December 20, 2010, https://www.9marks.org/article/whats-wrong-search-committees-part-1-2-finding-pastor/; and "What's Right about Elders? Part 2 of 2 on Finding a Pastor," 9Marks website, December 20, 2010, https://www.9marks.org/article/whats-right-about-elders-part-2-2-finding-pastor/.

2. Material in this section is adapted from Mark Dever, "Finding a Pastor," *Tabletalk*, August 2018, https://tabletalkmagazine.com/article/2018/08/finding-a-pastor/. Used with permission.

3. Quoted in Andrew Bonar, *Memoir and Remains of Robert Murray M'Cheyne* (Edinburgh: Banner of Truth, 1966), 185.

4. For more information about the Bible's teaching on elders, see Jeramie Rinne's book *Church Elders: How to Shepherd God's People Like Jesus* (Wheaton, IL: Crossway, 2014).

5. Charles Spurgeon, *The Soul Winner* (Grand Rapids, MI: Eerdmans, 1963), 37.
6. These steps are quoted from Dever, "Finding a Pastor."
7. For more questions along these lines, see articles "What Kind of Questions Should a Church Ask a Pastoral Candidate," and Paul Alexander, "Questions for Pastoral Candidates." Both are available at 9Marks.org.
8. Material in this section is adapted from Dever, "Finding a Pastor."
9. Edward Griffin, "A Tearful Farewell from a Faithful Pastor" (sermon, 1809).

Scripture Index

Scripture Index

 **9Marks**

Building Healthy Churches

9Marks exists to equip church leaders with a biblical vision and practical resources for displaying God's glory to the nations through healthy churches.

To that end, we want to see churches characterized by these nine marks of health:

1. Expositional Preaching
2. Biblical Theology
3. A Biblical Understanding of the Gospel
4. A Biblical Understanding of Conversion
5. A Biblical Understanding of Evangelism
6. Biblical Church Membership
7. Biblical Church Discipline
8. Biblical Discipleship
9. Biblical Church Leadership

Find all our Crossway titles and other resources at 9Marks.org.

9Marks | Church Questions

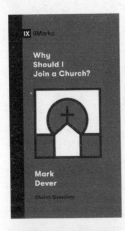

Why Should I Join a Church?

Mark Dever

Church Questions

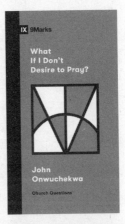

What If I Don't Desire to Pray?

John Onwuchekwa

Church Questions

What Should I Do Now That I'm a Christian?

Sam Emadi

Church Questions

What If I'm Discouraged in My Evangelism?

Isaac Adams

Church Questions

crossway.org